PATIENCE

PATIENCE

Warren W. Wiersbe

VICTOR BOOKS
A DIVISION OF SCRIPTURE PRESS PUBLICATIONS INC.
USA CANADA ENGLAND

All Scripture quotations are from the *Holy Bible: New International Version®*. Copyright © 1973, 1978, 1984 by International Bible Society. Used by permission of Zondervan Publishing House. All rights reserved.

Copyediting: Afton Rorvik
Cover Design: Grace K. Chan Mallette

Library of Congress Cataloging-in-Publication Data

Wiersbe, Warren W.
   Patience / by Warren W. Wiersbe.
     p.   cm.
   "Each devotional is adapted from a chapter in Be patient."
   1st prelim. page.
   ISBN 1-56476-400-1
   1. Bible. O.T. Job—Prayer-books and devotions—English.
2. Patience—Religious aspects—Christianity—Prayer-books and devotions—English. I. Wiersbe, Warren W. Be Patient. II. Title.
BS1415.4.W54 1995
223'.107—dc20   94-37697
                                                                                   CIP

© 1995 by Victor Books / SP Publications, Inc. All rights reserved. Printed in the United States of America.

1 2 3 4 5 6 7 8 9 10 Printing / Year 99 98 97 96 95

No part of this book may be reproduced without written permission, except for brief quotations in books and critical reviews. For information write Victor Books, 1825 College Avenue, Wheaton, Illinois 60187.

If you are studying *Be Patient* in a Sunday School class or small group, this 30-Day Devotional will complement your study. Each devotional is adapted from a chapter in *Be Patient*. The following chart indicates the correlation. You may, of course, use this book without reference to *Be Patient*.

Be Patient	**Patience**
Book Chapter	**30-Day Devotional**
Preface	**Day 1**
1	**Days 2, 3, 4, and 5**
2	**Day 6**
3	**Days 7 and 8**
4	**Days 9 and 10**
5	**Days 11 and 12**
6	**Days 13, 14, and 15**
7	**Days 16 and 17**
8	**Days 18 and 19**
9	**Days 20 and 21**
10	**Days 22 and 23**
11	**Days 24 and 25**
12	**Days 26 and 27**
13	**Days 28, 29, and 30**

INTRODUCTION

The only thing many of us know about patience is how to spell the word.

The Book of Job is the greatest book ever written on patience. Nobody in Bible history, except Jesus Christ, suffered more than Job, and because Job suffered, we can learn from him how to accept the tough experiences of life and profit from them. As you listen to Job's debates with his friends, and then hear the penetrating words of Jehovah, you can discover new depths of understanding about life and new facets of truth about yourself. Through it all, you can learn how to develop patience.

What life does *to* us depends on what life finds *in* us. The Book of Job challenges us to have faith in our hearts that the trials of life are appointments, not accidents, and that God does indeed work all things together for our good. When God puts us into the furnace, He keeps His eye on the clock and His hand on the thermostat, so we don't have to be afraid.

One more thing: whenever you ask God for patience, He usually sends trials. Be prepared. There are no shortcuts when it comes to building Christian character. But it's worth it to go through the furnace of suffering if, like Job, we can say "Though He slay me, yet will I hope in Him!" (Job 13:15) When that's your testimony, you'll come out of the furnace as pure gold.

That's what happened to Job, and it can happen to us.

—Warren W. Wiersbe

*My thanks to Stan Campbell,
who compiled the contents of this book
and added thought-provoking questions
to enrich your personal growth.*

DAY 1

*Read **James 5:11***

Ready to Suffer?

Many people have heard about Job and his trials; but not many people understand what those trials were all about and what God was trying to accomplish. Nor do they realize that Job suffered as he did so that God's people today might learn from his experiences how to be patient in suffering and endure to the end.

When I decided to write about Job, I said to my wife, "I wonder how much suffering we'll have to go through so I can write this book." Little did we realize the trials that God would permit us to experience! But we can testify that God is faithful, He answers prayer, and He always has a wonderful purpose in mind (Jer. 29:11).

You too may have to go through the furnace in order to study the Book of Job and really grasp its message. If so, don't be afraid! By faith, just say with Job, "He knows the way that I take; when He has tested me, I will come forth as gold" (Job 23:10). God fears no fire. Whatever we have that is burned up and left behind in the furnace wasn't worth having anyway.

As we study the Book of Job together, I trust that two things will be accomplished in your life: you will

> *"You have heard of Job's perseverance and have seen what the Lord finally brought about. The Lord is full of compassion and mercy"*
> *(James 5:11).*

....

learn to be patient in your own trials, and you will learn how to help others in their trials. Your world is filled with people who need encouragement, and God may be preparing you for just that ministry. Either way, I hope this book helps you.

Applying God's Truth:

1. What are some current situations you are facing that are causing you to suffer?

2. On a scale of 1 (least) to 10 (most), how severely would you say you have suffered in the past? What events have caused the most intense suffering?

3. What do you hope to discover as you go through the Book of Job?

DAY 2

*Read **Job 1:1-5***

Gritty Integrity

Lord Byron was on target when he wrote: "Truth is always strange; stranger than fiction."

The Book of Job is not religious fiction. Job was a real person, not an imaginary character; both Ezekiel (14:14, 20) and James (5:11) attest to that. Because he was a real man who had real experiences, he can tell us what we need to know about life and its problems in this real world.

Job was "blameless and upright." He was not sinless, for nobody can claim that distinction; but he was complete and mature in character and "straight" in conduct. The word translated "blameless" is related to "integrity," another important word throughout the Book of Job. People with integrity are whole persons, without hypocrisy or duplicity. In the face of his friends' accusations and God's silence, Job maintained his integrity; and the LORD ultimately vindicated him.

The foundation for Job's character was the fact that he "feared God and shunned evil." To fear the LORD means to respect who He is, what He says, and

> *"In the land of Uz there lived a man whose name was Job. This man was blameless and upright; he feared God and shunned evil"*
> *(Job 1:1).*

....

what He does. It is not the cringing fear of a slave before a master but the loving reverence of a child before a father; a respect that leads to obedience. "The remarkable thing about fearing God," said Oswald Chambers, "is that when you fear God you fear nothing else, whereas if you do not fear God you fear everything else."

Applying God's Truth:

1. What things would you need to do before other people considered you blameless?

2. Can you think of a recent situation where you considered compromising your integrity? If not, can you think of any situation where you might?

3. Would you say that you fear God? Explain.

DAY 3

*Read **Job 1:6-19***

First, the Bad News

In one day, Job was stripped of his wealth. One after another, four frightened messengers reported that 500 yoke of oxen, 500 donkeys, and 3,000 camels were stolen in enemy raids; 7,000 sheep were struck by lightning and killed; all 10 of his children were killed in a windstorm.

Job knew *what* had happened, but he did not know *why* it had happened, and that is the crux of the matter. Because the author allows us to visit the throne room of heaven and hear God and Satan speak, we know who caused the destruction and why he was allowed to cause it. But if we did not have this insight, we would probably take the same approach as Job's friends and blame Job for the tragedy.

Several important truths emerge from this scene, not the least of which is that *God is sovereign in all things.* He is on the throne of heaven, the angels do His will and report to Him, and even Satan can do nothing to God's people without God's permission. "The Almighty" is one of the key names for God in Job; it is used thirty-one times. From the outset, the writer reminds us that, no matter what happens in this world

> *"Yet another messenger came and said, 'Your sons and daughters were feasting . . . when suddenly a mighty wind swept in from the desert and struck the four corners of the house. It collapsed on them and they are dead' "*
> *(Job 1:18-19).*

and in our lives, God is on the throne and has everything under control.

We may not know until we get to heaven why God allowed certain things to happen. Meanwhile, we walk by faith and say with Job, "May the name of the LORD be praised" (Job 1:21).

Applying God's Truth:

1. If the devastating events of Job's life happened to you today, what do you think you would do? Be specific.

2. How would these events make you feel about God? (Be truthful.)

3. When you get to heaven, what is one thing you would like to ask God?

DAY 4

Read **Job 1:20-22**

Worst of Times, Worship Times

The hosts of heaven and of hell watched to see how Job would respond to the loss of his wealth and his children. He expressed his grief in a manner normal for that day, for God expects us to be human (1 Thes. 4:13). After all, even Jesus wept (John 11:35). But then Job worshiped God and uttered a profound statement of faith.

First, he looked back to his birth: "Naked I came from my mother's womb." Everything Job owned was given to him by God, and the same God who gave it had the right to take it away. Job simply acknowledged that he was a steward.

Then Job looked ahead to his death: "and naked I will depart." He would not return to his mother's womb because that would be impossible. He would go to "Mother Earth," be buried, and turn to dust. Nothing that he acquired between his birth and death would go with him into the next world.

Finally, Job looked up and uttered a magnificent statement of faith: "The LORD gave and the LORD has taken away; may the name of the LORD be praised."

> *"The LORD gave and the LORD has taken away; may the name of the LORD be praised"*
> *(Job 1:21).*

....

Instead of cursing God, as Satan said Job would do, Job blessed the LORD! Anybody can say, "The LORD gave" or "The LORD has taken away," but it takes real faith to say in the midst of sorrow and suffering, "May the name of the LORD be praised."

Applying God's Truth:

1. Do you think Job's worship during his great tragedy suggests that he was in denial of his situation? Explain.

2. Do you think Job's actions were appropriate? Why?

3. What are some less effective responses to tragedy that people use today?

DAY 5

Read *Job 2–3*

Three Heads Are No Better Than One

You will be spending a good deal of time with Job's three friends, so you had better get acquainted with them.

All three of the men were old (Job 32:6), older than Job (15:10), but we assume that *Eliphaz* was the oldest. He is named first (2:11), he spoke first, and the Lord seems to have accepted him as the elder member of the trio (42:7). Eliphaz put great faith in tradition (15:18-19), and the God he worshiped was an inflexible Lawgiver. He had a rigid theology that left little or no room for the grace of God.

Bildad must have been the second oldest of the three since he is named second and spoke after Eliphaz. In a word, Bildad was a *legalist*. For some reason, Bildad was sure that Job's children died because they also were sinners (v. 4). The man seemed to have no feeling for his hurting friend.

Zophar was the youngest of the three and surely the most dogmatic. He spoke like a schoolmaster addressing a group of ignorant freshmen. "Know this!" is his unfeeling approach. He was merciless and told

> *"When Job's three friends . . . heard about all the troubles that had come upon him, they set out from their homes and met together by agreement to go and sympathize with him and comfort him"*
> *(Job 2:11).*

....

Job that God was giving him far less than he deserved for his sins! (11:6) Interestingly enough, Zophar spoke to Job only twice. Either he decided he was unable to answer Job's arguments or felt that it was a waste of time trying to help Job.

All three men said true things, as well as foolish things; but they didn't help Job because their viewpoint was too narrow. These men perfectly illustrate Dorothy Sayers' statement, "There's nothing you can't prove if your outlook is sufficiently limited."

Applying God's Truth:

1. When you have serious problems, what three friends do you most trust for advice?

2. Do you have "friends" like Job's, who offer advice with little if any sensitivity? How do you respond to their advice?

3. What can you learn about being a friend from Eliphaz, Bildad, and Zophar?

DAY 6

Read **Job 4—5**

A Word from the Unwise

Job's three friends were silent for seven days (Job 2:13), and Job later wished they had stayed that way (13:5). Then Eliphaz the Temanite answered Job. But what did he answer? The pain in Job's heart? No, he answered the words from Job's lips; and *this was a mistake*. A wise counselor and comforter must listen with the heart and respond to feelings as well as to words. You do not heal a broken heart with logic; you heal a broken heart with love. Yes, you must speak the truth; but be sure to speak the truth in love (Eph. 4:15).

Eliphaz's approach seems to start out positively enough, even gently; but it was only honey to prepare Job for the bitterness that would follow. "Don't get upset, Job!" is what he was saying. "In the past your words have been a help to many people; and we want our words to be a help to you."

Never underestimate the power of words to encourage people in the battles of life. James Moffat translates Job 4:4, "Your words have kept men on their feet." The right words, spoken at the right time, and with the right motive, can make a tremendous

> *"Then Eliphaz the Temanite replied:*
> *'If someone ventures a word with you,*
> *will you be impatient? But who*
> *can keep from speaking?'"*
>
> *(Job 4:1-2)*

....

difference in the lives of others. Your words can nourish those who are weak and encourage those who are defeated. But your words can also hurt those who are broken and only add to their burdens, so be careful what you say and how you say it.

Applying God's Truth:

1. What do you suppose Job's friends were thinking during their seven days of silence?

2. Can you think of a recent time when you responded to someone's *words* rather than his or her *feelings*? How might you have improved your response?

3. When was a time that you felt you comforted someone with the right words, at the right time, and with the right motive?

DAY 7

Read **Job 6–8**

Defending Justice, Forgetting Love

"Your words are a blustering wind." Can you imagine a counselor saying that to a suffering individual who wanted to die? Bildad did; in fact, he used the same approach in his next speech (18:2). Job had poured out his grief and was waiting to hear a sympathetic word, but his friend said that Job's speech was just so much hot air.

There is a reason for Bildad's approach: he was so concerned about defending the justice of God that he forgot the needs of his friend. While Bildad's theology was correct — God is just — his application of that theology was wrong. Bildad was looking at only one aspect of God's nature — His holiness and justice — and had forgotten His love, mercy, and goodness. Yes, "God is light" (1 John 1:5), but don't forget that "God is love" (4:8, 16). His love is a holy love, and His holiness is exercised in love, even when He judges sin.

How are these two attributes of God reconciled? At the Cross. When Jesus died for the sins of the world, the righteousness of God was vindicated, for sin was judged; but the love of God was demonstrated, for a Savior was provided. At Calvary, God was both "just

> *"Then Bildad the Shuhite replied:*
> *'How long will you say such things?*
> *Your words are a blustering wind' "*
> *(Job 8:1-2).*

and the one who justifies" (Rom. 3:24-26). God's law said, "The soul who sins is the one who will die" (Ezek. 18:4, 20); and God obeyed His own law in the sacrificing of His Son on the cross. In Christ's resurrection, the grace of God triumphed over sin and death, and all who repent of their sins and trust Jesus Christ will be saved.

Applying God's Truth:

1. What problems might people expect who focus too much on God's justice without considering His great love?

2. What problems might people expect who concentrate on God's love while ignoring His holy justice?

3. What steps can you take to ensure that you maintain a sense of God's love *and* justice as you advise and console others?

DAY 8

Read *Job 9—10*

An Offering of Suffering

In Job 9 and 10, Job asks three questions: (1) "How can I be righteous before God" (9:1-13); (2) "How can I meet God in court?" (vv. 14-35); and (3) "Why was I born?" (10:1-22; see v. 18). You can see how these questions connect. Job is righteous, but he has to prove it. How can a mortal man prove himself righteous before God? Can he take God to court? But if God doesn't step in and testify on Job's behalf, what is the purpose of all this suffering? Why was Job even born?

Job could not understand what God was doing, *and it was important that he not understand.* Had Job known that God was using him as a weapon to defeat Satan, he could have simply sat back and waited trustfully for the battle to end. But as Job surveyed himself and his situation, he asked the same question the disciples asked when Mary anointed the Lord Jesus: "Why this waste?" (Mark 14:4) Before we criticize Job too severely, let's recall how many times we have asked that question ourselves when a baby has died or a promising young person was killed in an accident.

> *"Though I were innocent, I could not answer Him; I could only plead with my Judge for mercy"*
> *(Job 9:15).*

....

Nothing that is given to Christ in faith and love is ever wasted. The fragrance of Mary's ointment faded from the scene centuries ago, but the significance of her worship has blessed Christians in every age and continues to do so. Job was bankrupt and sick, and all he could give to the LORD was his suffering by faith; *but that is just what God wanted in order to silence the devil.*

Applying God's Truth:

1. What top three questions about life and God are you currently struggling with?

2. Can you think of an event in the past when you couldn't understand what God was doing (or why), but later were able to see His plan clearly?

3. Mary offered ointment. Job offered suffering. Can you think of something equally unusual or unique to offer God?

DAY 9

Read **Job 11**

Zophar So Good?

Zophar makes three accusations against Job: Job is guilty of sin (Job 11:1-4); Job is ignorant of God (vv. 5-12); and Job is stubborn in his refusal to repent (vv. 13-20).

"There is hope!" is Zophar's encouraging word to Job, and he described what Job could experience. But if Job wanted these blessings, he had to get them on Zophar's terms. Yes, there was hope, but it was hope with a condition attached to it: Job must repent and confess his sins (vv. 13-14). *Zophar is tempting Job to bargain with God so he can get out of his troubles.* This is exactly what Satan wanted Job to do!

"Does Job fear God for nothing?" Satan asked (1:9). Satan accused Job of having a "commercial faith" that promised prosperity in return for obedience. If Job had followed Zophar's advice, he would have played right into the hands of the enemy.

Job did not have a "commercial faith" that made bargains with God. He had a confident faith that said, "Though He slay me, yet will I hope in Him" (13:15). That doesn't sound like a man looking for an easy way

> *"If you put away the sin that is in your hand and allow no evil to dwell in your tent, then you will lift up your face without shame; you will stand firm and without fear"*
> *(Job 11:14-15).*

out of difficulties. "Job did not understand the Lord's reasons," said C. H. Spurgeon, "but he continued to confide in His goodness." That is faith!

Applying God's Truth:

1. What have people recently accused you of? How did each accusation make you feel?

2. In what ways do people today attempt to bargain with God?

3. How would you feel if you were in Job's place and heard the accusations and advice of Zophar?

DAY 10

Read *Job 12–14*

Appealing to a Higher Court

Job 13:13-17 is one of the greatest declarations of faith found anywhere in Scripture, but it must be understood in its context. Job is saying, "I will take my case directly to God and prove my integrity. I know I am taking my life in my hands in approaching God because He is able to slay me. But if He doesn't slay me, it is proof that I am not the hypocrite you say I am." Later, Job will take an oath and challenge God to pass judgment (Job 27). To approach God personally was a great act of faith, but Job was so sure of his integrity that he would take his chances. After all, if he did nothing, he would die. And if he were rejected by God, he would die, but there was always the possibility that God would prove him right.

Why does Job want to meet God in court? So that God can once and for all state His "case" against Job and let Job know the sins in his life that have caused him to suffer so much. "Why should God pay so much attention to me?" asks Job. "He treats me like an enemy, but I'm just a weak leaf in the wind, a piece of chaff that is worth nothing. I'm a piece of rotting wood and a moth-eaten garment, yet God treats me like a prisoner of war and watches me every minute" (13:24-

> *"Though He slay me, yet will I hope in Him;
> I will surely defend my ways to His face"*
> *(Job 13:15).*

28). Job felt the time had come to settle the matter, even if it meant losing his own life in the process.

Applying God's Truth:

1. What do you think about Job's desire to meet God "in court"?

2. Have you ever felt so righteous and innocent that you would invite God to check you out personally? Explain.

3. What do you think motivated Job's actions: Desperation? Confidence? Or something else?

DAY 11

Read *Job 15*

You Get What You Deserve?

In his first speech Eliphaz had described the blessings of the godly man (5:17-26), but now he describes the sufferings of the ungodly man. The problem with Eliphaz's statement about the judgment of the wicked is that *it is not always true in this life.* Many wicked people go through life apparently happy and successful, while many godly people experience suffering and seeming failure. It is true that *ultimately* the wicked suffer and the godly are blessed, but, meanwhile, it often looks like the situation is reversed (Ps. 73; Jer. 12:1-4). Furthermore, God gives sunshine to the evil and the good and sends rain on the just and the unjust (Matt. 5:45). He is long-suffering toward sinners (2 Peter 3:9) and waits for His goodness to lead them to repentance (Rom. 2:4; Luke 15:17-19).

The greatest judgment God could send to the wicked in this life would be to *let them have their own way.* "They have their reward" (Matt. 6:2, 5, 16). The only heaven the godless will know is the enjoyment they have on earth in this life, and God is willing for them to have it. The only suffering the godly will experience is in this life, for in heaven there will be no

> *"All his days the wicked man suffers torment, the ruthless through all the years stored up for him"*
> (Job 15:20).

....

pain or tears. Furthermore, the suffering that God's people experience now is working for them and will one day lead to glory (1 Peter 1:6-8; 5:10; 2 Cor. 4:16-18; Rom. 8:18). Eliphaz and his friends had the situation all confused.

Applying God's Truth:

1. Do you ever agree with Eliphaz's opinion, expressed in today's key verse? Why?

2. How many cases can you think of where a righteous person you know is experiencing major suffering? How about wicked people who seem to prosper?

3. The next time you suffer unfairly, what might you remember to help you endure the situation?

DAY 12

Read *Job 16–17*

Nothing Left to Live For

Job's friends were against him and would not go to court and "post bond" for him (Job 17:3-5). People treated Job as if he were the scum of the earth (v. 6). His body was only the shadow of what it had been (v. 7), and all of his plans had been shattered (v. 11). His friends would not change their minds and come to his defense (v. 10). In fact, they would not face his situation honestly, but they kept telling him that the light would soon dawn for him (v. 12). Is it any wonder that Job saw in death the only way of escape?

God did not answer Job's plea for death because He had something far better planned for him. God looked beyond Job's depression and bitterness and saw that he still had faith. When I was a young pastor, I heard an experienced saint say, "I have lived long enough to be thankful for unanswered prayer." At the time I was shocked by the statement, but now that I have lived a few more years myself, I know what she was talking about. In the darkness of despair and the prison of pain, we often say things that we later regret; *but God understands all about it and lovingly turns a deaf ear to our words but a tender eye to our wounds.*

"If the only home I hope for is the grave . . . where then is my hope?"
(Job 17:13, 15)

Applying God's Truth:

1. Have you ever felt that you had little, if anything, to live for? If so, what were the circumstances? If not, what's the worst you've ever felt (emotionally)?

2. How might Job's friends have affected his outlook in a more positive way?

3. Can you think of an unanswered prayer in your past for which you're thankful?

DAY 13

*Read **Job 18***

Fear As a Motivator

In Bildad's second speech, his weapon was *fear*. If the three friends could not reason with Job, or shame Job into repenting, perhaps they could frighten Job by describing what happens when wicked people die. However, Bildad made two mistakes when he gave this speech about the horrors of death. To begin with, he preached it to the wrong man; for Job was already a believer (Job 1:1, 8). Second, he preached it with the wrong motive, for there was no love in his heart. Dr. R.W. Dale, the British preacher, once asked evangelist D.L. Moody if he ever used "the element of terror" in his preaching. Moody replied that he usually preached one sermon on heaven and one on hell in each of his campaigns, but that a "man's heart ought to be very tender" when preaching about the doom of the lost. Bildad did not have a very tender heart.

Though Bildad was talking to the wrong man and with the wrong motive, what he said about death should be taken seriously. Death is an enemy to be feared by all who are not prepared to die (1 Cor. 15:26), and the only way to be prepared is to trust Jesus Christ (John 5:24).

> *"The lamp of the wicked is snuffed out;*
> *the flame of his fire stops burning"*
> *(Job 18:5).*

....

For the Christian believer, death means going home to the Father in heaven (John 14:1-6), falling asleep on earth and waking up in heaven (Acts 7:60; Phil. 1:21-23), entering into rest (Rev. 14:13), and moving into greater light (Prov. 4:18). None of the pictures Bildad used (Job 18:5-21) should be applied to those who have trusted the Lord for salvation.

Applying God's Truth:

1. Has anyone ever tried to use fear to motivate you into being a better person or better Christian? How well did the appeal work?

2. What are some other "motivators" people use with the wrong motives?

3. Think of your own recent interactions with friends and family members. Can you think of any instances where you have tried to influence others with improper motives or tactics?

DAY 14

Read **Job 19:1-20**

Darkness on a Dead-end Street

Job saw himself as a traveler fenced in. Satan had complained that God had "walled in" Job and his family so that they were protected from trouble (1:9-12). Now Job is complaining because God has blocked his path, and he cannot move. Job could not see what lay ahead because God had shrouded the way with darkness.

At times God permits His children to experience darkness on a dead-end street where they don't know which way to turn. When this happens, *wait for the Lord to give you light in His own time.* Don't try to manufacture your own light or to borrow light from others.

Dr. Bob Jones, Sr. used to say, "Never doubt in the darkness what God has taught you in the light." In fact, what God teaches us in the light will become even more meaningful in the darkness.

"Oh, the unspeakable benediction of the 'treasures of darkness'!" wrote Oswald Chambers. "It is not the days of sunshine and splendor and liberty and light that leave their lasting and indelible effect upon the

> *"He has blocked my way so I cannot pass;*
> *He has shrouded my paths in darkness"*
> *(Job 19:8).*

....

soul, but those nights of the Spirit in which, shadowed by God's hand, hidden in the dark cleft of some rock in a weary land, He lets the splendors of the outskirts of Himself pass before our gaze."

Applying God's Truth:

1. How do you tend to react when God chooses not to reveal what lies ahead for you?

2. On a scale of 1 (least) to 10 (most), how strong is your faith "in the darkness"? How could it be stronger?

3. What have you discovered about God during difficult times that you might not otherwise have noticed?

DAY 15

Read *Job 19:21-29*

Carved in Stone

Why, in today's reading, did Job want his words to be recorded permanently? He thought he was going to die before God would vindicate him, and he wanted people to remember how he suffered and what he said. Bildad warned him, "The memory of [a wicked man] perishes from the earth" (18:17), and Job wanted his record to remain.

At this point, Job uttered another of his statements of faith that in this book punctuate his many expressions of grief and pain. It is significant that Job would go from the depths of despair to the heights of faith, and then back into the depths again. *This is often the normal experience of people experiencing great suffering.*

In spite of what some preachers say, very few people can maintain a constant high level of faith and courage in times of severe pain and trial. John Henry Jowett, at one time known as "the greatest preacher in the English-speaking world," wrote to a friend: "I wish you wouldn't think I am such a saint. You seem to imagine that I have no ups and downs, but just a level and lofty stretch of spiritual attainment with unbroken

> *"I know that my Redeemer lives, and that in the end He will stand upon the earth"*
> *(Job 19:25).*

....

joy and equanimity. By no means! I am often perfectly wretched, and everything appears most murky" (*John Henry Jowett*, by Arthur Porrit, p. 290).

Job expressed confidence that, even if he died, he would still have a Redeemer who one day would exercise judgment on the earth. Furthermore, Job affirmed that he himself expected to live again and see his Redeemer! It was an affirmation of faith in the resurrection of the human body.

Applying God's Truth:

1. What truths do you so strongly believe about God that they could be recorded permanently — "carved in stone," so to speak?

2. Are you as open about the "lows" of your spiritual life as you are the "highs"? Do you think you *should* be?

3. What are the benefits of having confidence in a living Redeemer?

DAY 16

Read **Job 20:1–21:6**

Now Ear This

Listen to Job's appeal to his friends that they try to understand how he feels. "If you really want to console me, just keep quiet and listen" (21:2, paraphrase). The Greek philosopher Zeno said, "The reason why we have two ears and only one mouth is that we may listen the more and talk the less." The friends thought their words would encourage Job, but he said that their silence would encourage him even more (13:3).

Job pointed out that his complaint was not against men but against God. Men had not caused his afflictions, and men could not take them away. If he was impatient, it was because God had not answered him (v. 3). The longer God waited, the worse Job's situation became. "Look at me and be astonished; clap your hand over your mouth" (21:5).

As Job contemplated what he was about to say, it stirred him to the depths (v. 6). This was no speech from "off the top of his head," for it had to do with the basic facts of life and death. If Job's friends were in his situation, they would see things differently and *say* things differently.

> *"Listen carefully to my words; let this be the consolation you give me"*
> *(Job 21:2).*

Applying God's Truth:

1. Can you think of someone to whom you could minister simply by *listening* to him or her?

2. Job's friends were trying to be helpful. Why don't you think Job appreciated their words?

3. How can you remember to show more empathy the next time you're in a position to advise or console someone?

DAY 17

*Read **Job 21:7-34***

Lifestyle Envy
....

The saddest thing about the wicked is the way they leave God out of their lives and still prosper (21:14-15). The wicked take credit for their wealth, but Job acknowledged that everything comes from God (1:21). How, then, can Job's three friends classify him with the wicked?

We must face the disturbing fact that too many professed Christians actually admire and envy the lifestyle of the rich and famous. In one of his books, Dr. Kenneth Chafin tells about a pastor and deacon who were visiting prospects and stopped at a beautiful suburban home. The lawn looked manicured, and two expensive cars sat in the driveway. Furthermore, the pastor and deacon could see the man of the house comfortably seated in his spacious living room, watching television. Everything about the place reeked of affluence. The deacon turned to his pastor and asked, "What kind of good news do we have for this fellow?"

In over forty years of ministry, I have performed many weddings and watched many young Christian couples get started in their homes. What a joy it has

> *"Their prosperity is not in their own hands, so I stand aloof from the counsel of the wicked"*
> *(Job 21:16).*

been to see homes where couples set the right priorities and resist the temptation to "follow the crowd" and live for material possessions. Unfortunately, some have lost their spiritual vision and succeeded in this world — without acknowledging the Lord. Alas, they have their reward.

Applying God's Truth:

1. Does anything ever cause you to be jealous of others? (Bigger homes? Better cars?)

2. How do you deal with twinges of jealousy when they come?

3. How do you think God feels when His people succumb to jealousy of others' material possessions?

DAY 18

*Read **Job 22***

The Slanderers of Uz

What should have been an encouraging discussion among friends had become an angry and painful debate. Instead of trying to calm things down, Eliphaz assumed the office of prosecuting attorney and turned the debate into a trial. It was three against one as Job sat on the ash heap and listened to his friends lie about him. According to the Jewish Talmud, "The slanderous tongue kills three: the slandered, the slanderer, and him who listens to the slander." At the ash heap in Uz, it was death all around!

Eliphaz first accused Job of the sin of pride (22:1-3). Job was acting as though his character and conduct were important to God and beneficial to Him in some way. Eliphaz's theology centered around a distant God who was the Judge of the world but not the Friend of sinners.

But Job's character and conduct were important to God, for *God was using Job to silence the devil.* Neither Job nor his three friends knew God's hidden plan, but Job had faith to believe that God was achieving some purpose in his life and would one day vindicate him. Furthermore, the character and

> *"Is it for your piety that He rebukes you*
> *and brings charges against you?*
> *Is not your wickedness great?*
> *Are not your sins endless?"*
>
> *(Job 22:4-5)*

behavior of God's people *are* important to the Lord because His people bring Him either joy or sorrow (1 Thes. 4:1; Heb. 11:5; Gen. 6:5-6; Ps. 37:23). He is not a passive, distant God who does not identify with His people, but the God who delights in them as they delight in Him (Ps. 18:19; Isa. 63:9; Heb. 4:14-16).

Applying God's Truth:

1. How do you tend to react when people make false accusations against you?

2. How do you handle those times when you *know* you're right, but are outnumbered by people who disagree with you?

3. Can you think of how any unpleasant circumstances you're currently facing might be part of God's "hidden plan"?

DAY 19

Read Job 23–24

The Greater the Heat, the Purer the Gold

God knew where Job was—in the furnace! But it was a furnace of God's appointment, not because of Job's sin; God would use Job's affliction to purify him and make him a better man. This is not the only answer to the question, "Why do the righteous suffer?" but it is one of the best, and it can bring the sufferer great encouragement.

Scripture often uses the image of a furnace to describe God's purifying ministry through suffering (Isa. 48:10; Deut 4:20; Ps. 66:10). The image is also used in 1 Peter 1:6-7 and 4:12 of believers going through persecution.

When God puts His own people into the furnace, He keeps His eye on the clock and His hand on the thermostat. He knows how long and how much. We may question why He does it to begin with, or why He doesn't turn down the heat or even turn it off, but our questions are only evidences of unbelief. Job 23:10 is the answer: "He knows the way that I take; when He has tested me, I will come forth as gold." *Gold does not fear the fire.* The furnace can only make the gold purer and brighter.

> *"He knows the way that I take; when He has tested me, I will come forth as gold"*
> *(Job 23:10).*

....
Applying God's Truth:

1. Before today's reading, what would you have said if a friend asked, "Why do you think good people are allowed to suffer?"

2. Do you try to avoid the heat of "God's furnace," or do you allow hard times to purify you? Give some examples.

3. Do you trust God *completely* to protect you during your "furnace experiences"? Why or why not?

DAY 20

Read *Job 25—26*

On the Fringe

Bildad's speech in Job 25 is the shortest in the book and focuses on God's power (vv. 1-3) and justice (vv. 4-6). It is disturbing to see how Job's friends speak so knowingly about God when, in the end, God revealed that they really didn't know what they were talking about. Too often, those who say the most about God know the least about God.

Job first rebuked Bildad for giving him no help (26:1-4). Then Job extolled the greatness of God (vv. 5-13). The three friends must have listened impatiently because they already knew the things Job was talking about, *but they hadn't drawn the right conclusion from them.* Because they saw God's handiwork in nature, they thought they knew all about God; therefore they could explain God to Job.

Job said that just the opposite was true (v. 14). What we see of God in creation is but the fringes of His ways, and what we hear is but a whisper of His power! Knowing a few facts about the creation of God is not the same as knowing truths about the God of Creation.

The fourteenth-century British spiritual writer

> *"These are but the outer fringe of His works; how faint the whisper we hear of Him! Who then can understand the thunder of His power?"*
> *(Job 26:14)*

....

Richard Rolle said, "He truly knows God perfectly that finds Him incomprehensible and unable to be known." The more we learn about God, the more we discover how much more there is to know! Beware of people who claim to know all about God, for their claim is proof they know neither God nor themselves.

Applying God's Truth:

1. How do you respond to people who claim to speak for God, yet obviously don't reflect His love or knowledge?

2. Think of everything you *do* know about God. What percentage of His fullness do you think your knowledge would comprise?

3. What are some things you could do to: (1) Know God more completely, and (2) Better represent Him to others?

DAY 21

Read **Job 27–28**

The Beginning of Wisdom

The first step toward true wisdom is a reverent and respectful attitude toward God, which also involves a humble attitude toward ourselves. *Personal pride is the greatest barrier to spiritual wisdom.* "When pride comes, then comes disgrace, but with humility comes wisdom" (Prov. 11:2).

The next step is to ask God for wisdom (James 1:5) and make diligent use of the means He gives us for securing His wisdom, especially knowing and doing the Word of God (Matt. 7:21-29). It is not enough merely to study; we must also obey what God tells us to do (John 7:17). As we walk by faith, we discover the wisdom of God in the everyday things of life. Spiritual wisdom is not abstract; it is very personal and very practical.

As we fellowship with other believers in the church and share with one another, we can learn wisdom. Reading the best books can also help us grow in wisdom and understanding. The important thing is that we focus on Christ, for He is our wisdom (1 Cor. 1:24) and in Him is hidden "all the treasures of wisdom and knowledge" (Col. 2:3). The better we

> *"The fear of the Lord—that is wisdom,
> and to shun evil is understanding"*
> *(Job 28:28).*

know Christ and the more we become like Him, the more we will walk in wisdom and understand the will of the Lord. We must allow the Holy Spirit to open the eyes of our heart so we can see God in His Word and understand more of the riches we have in Christ (Eph. 1:15-23).

Applying God's Truth:

1. In what ways is personal pride a potential barrier for your own accumulation of spiritual wisdom?

2. What are some *specific* situations for which you need to ask God for additional wisdom?

3. Can you think of any good *human* resources to help provide wisdom for the situations you've listed?

DAY 22

*Read **Job 29***

Gone but Not Forgotten

Job had opened his defense by saying that he wished he had never been born (Job 3). Now he closed his defense by remembering the blessings he and his family had enjoyed prior to his crisis. This is a good reminder that we should try to see life in a balanced way. Yes, God permits us to experience difficulties and sorrows, but God also sends victories and joys. "Shall we accept good from God, and not trouble?" (2:10) C.H. Spurgeon said that too many people write their blessings in the sand but engrave their sorrows in marble.

"How I long for the months gone by, for the days when God watched over me!" When we are experiencing trials, it's natural for us to long for "the good old days," but our longing will not change our situation. Someone has defined "the good old days" as "a combination of a bad memory and a good imagination." In Job's case, however, his memory was accurate, and "the good old days" really were good.

There is a ministry in memory if we use it properly. In days of disappointment, it's good to "remember the deeds of the LORD . . . remember Your miracles of long

> *"How I long for the months gone by,*
> *for the days when God watched over me"*
> *(Job 29:2).*

....

ago" (Ps. 77:11). But the past must be a rudder to guide us and not an anchor to hold us back. If we try to duplicate today what we experienced yesterday, we may find ourselves in a rut that robs us of maturity.

Applying God's Truth:

1. Have you ever wished you had never been born? If yes, what caused your feelings?

2. What are some potential drawbacks to being nostalgic and thinking about "the good old days"?

3. How can your memory be a "ministry" to you or someone else?

DAY 23

Read **Job 30**

Mud-Wrestling with God

Job experienced sufferings similar to those of our Lord Jesus Christ. In the daytime, Job endured unbearable suffering; at night, God wrestled with him, made his clothing like a straitjacket, and threw him in the mud. Every night, God wrestled with Job; Job lost.

Job prayed to God. He even stood up and cried out for deliverance, but his prayers were unanswered (v. 20). Instead of God's hand bringing help, it only attacked Job ruthlessly and tossed him about like a feather in a storm (vv. 21-22). Job begged for his life, but death seemed inevitable (1:23).

Job had faithfully helped others in their need (29:12-17), but now nobody would help him. They wouldn't weep with him or even touch him. He was treated like a leper who might contaminate them, or like a condemned man whom God might destroy at any time. It just wasn't wise to get too close.

Where were the people that Job had helped? Surely some of them would have wanted to show their appreciation by encouraging their benefactor in his time of need. But nobody came to his aid. Mark Twain

> *"In His great power God becomes like clothing to me; He binds me like the neck of my garment. He throws me into the mud, and I am reduced to dust and ashes"*
> *(Job 30:18-19).*

....

wrote, "If you pick up a starving dog and make him prosperous, he will not bite you. This is the principal difference between a dog and a man." But according to missionary doctor Wilfred Grenfell, "The service we render for others is really the rent we pay for our room on this earth."

Applying God's Truth:

1. Has it ever seemed that God must have some kind of personal grudge against you?

2. After you help others, but they neglect to help you in return, how is your attitude toward service affected? (Do you allow the negligence of others to affect *your* ministry?)

3. Are you as honest about your feelings toward God as Job is in 30:18-23? Why or why not?

DAY 24

Read *Job 31—32:1*

Eli-Who?

Job was silent. He had ended his defense and given oath that he was not guilty of the sins he had been accused of by his friends. Job had challenged God either to vindicate him or pass sentence on him.

Job's three friends were silent, appalled that Job had dared to speak so boldly *to* God and *about* God.

God was silent. No fire came from heaven, and no voice spoke in divine wrath. The silence was God's eloquent witness to the three friends that they were wrong in what they had said both about Job and about God.

However, in the crowd around the ash heap, one person was not silent. It was Elihu, a man so unknown that his full pedigree had to be given so people could identify him (Job 32:2). While Elihu said some of the same things as the other speakers, his purpose was different from theirs. He was not trying to prove that Job was a sinner, but that Job's view of God was wrong. Elihu introduced a new truth into the debate: that God sends suffering, not necessarily to punish us for our sins, but to keep us from sinning (33:18, 24)

> *"So these three men stopped answering Job,
> because he was righteous in his own eyes"*
> *(Job 32:1).*

and to make us better persons (36:1-15). Paul would have agreed with the first point (2 Cor. 12:7-10) and the writer of Hebrews with the second (Heb. 12:1-11).

Applying God's Truth:

1. After Job had debated his three friends and poured his heart out to God, how do you think he felt when he heard silence rather than answers?

2. How would you have felt in his place to discover that yet another person had opinions to offer — and that he was just getting started?

3. Even though Elihu was making valid observations, do you think Job was taking them to heart? Why or why not?

DAY 25

Read *Job 32:2–33*

Sounds and Silence

Four times we are told that Elihu was angry. He was angry at the three friends for not refuting Job, and he was angry at Job for justifying himself rather than God. Job claimed that God was wrong, and the three friends couldn't prove that Job was wrong! Bildad, Zophar, and Eliphaz had given up the cause (32:15) and were waiting for God to come and deal personally with Job (vv. 12-13). Elihu was disgusted at their failure.

"It is easy to fly into a passion—anybody can do that," wrote Aristotle. "But to be angry with the right person to the right extent and at the right time and with the right object and in the right way—that is not easy, and it is not everyone who can do it."

Elihu promised Job that God would radically alter his situation if only he would humble himself. It would be like a "new birth"! (33:25) He would once more enjoy prayer and fellowship with God (33:26). He would confess his sins and admit that God had punished him far less than he deserved (v. 27). Job would move out of the darkness into the light and gladly bear witness of God's redemption (v. 28).

> *"But Elihu . . . became very angry with Job for justifying himself rather than God"*
> *(Job 32:2).*

Job 33:31-33 suggests that Elihu wanted Job's response, but at the same time Elihu wanted Job to keep quiet! Elihu was filled to the brim with his subject and didn't want to stop talking. But Job didn't reply because he was waiting for God to speak. Job had already stated his case and thrown down the gauntlet. What Elihu thought about him or said to him made little difference to Job.

Job had taken his case to a much higher court; when Elihu finishes speaking, the Judge will appear.

Applying God's Truth:

1. Do you think anger ever affects your ministry to others? In what specific ways?

2. When was the last time you felt you were angry "with the right person to the right extent and at the right time and with the right object and in the right way"?

3. Is it easy for you to ignore someone who is very angry? What do you think Job's lack of response to Elihu indicated about his mind-set?

DAY 26

Read *Job 34—35*

Defending God

Theology ("the science of God") used to be called "the queen of sciences" because it deals with the most important knowledge we can have, the knowledge of God. Theology is a necessary science, but it is also a difficult science; it is our attempt to know the Unknowable (Rom. 11:33-36). God has revealed Himself in creation, in providence, in His Word, and supremely in His Son, but our understanding of what God has revealed may not always be clear.

"The essence of idolatry," wrote A. W. Tozer, "is the entertainment of thoughts about God that are unworthy of Him" (*The Knowledge of the Holy*, Harper and Row, p. 11). So, whoever attempts to explain and defend the Almighty must have the humble heart of a worshiper, for "knowledge puffs up, but love builds up" (1 Cor. 8:1).

As you read Elihu's speeches, you get the impression that he was not growing; he was swelling. You also get the impression that his listeners' minds were wandering, because he kept exhorting them to listen carefully (Job 33:1, 31, 33; 34:2, 10, 16).

> *"Listen to me, you men of understanding.*
> *Far be it from God to do evil, from the*
> *Almighty to do wrong"*
> *(Job 34:10).*

Yet Elihu emphasized that God is sovereign, and the Book of Job magnifies the sovereignty of God. From the very first chapter, it is obvious that God is in control; even Satan is told what he can and cannot do. During the debate, it appears that God is absent, but He is aware of how Job feels and what Job and his friends say. Elihu was right on target: God is sovereign and cannot do wrong.

Applying God's Truth:

1. What are some theological questions that have come up in your interactions with skeptics or people of other faiths?

2. Do you know religious people who are "all theory and no practicality"? How might people avoid such a problem?

3. Even though Elihu was "right on target," do you think Job benefited from his words? Why or why not?

DAY 27

Read **Job 36–37**

A Helpful, but Overlooked, Ministry

Elihu urged Job to catch a new vision of the greatness of God and start praising Him (36:22-25). God wants to teach us through our sufferings (v. 22), and one evidence that we are learning our lessons is that we praise and thank Him, even for trials. "Remember to extol His work, which men have praised in song" (v. 24). "Praise changes things" just as much as "prayer changes things."

With all his verbosity and lack of humility, Elihu did say some good things that Job needed to hear. Elihu's use of rhetorical questions in 37:14-18 prepared Job for the series of questions Jehovah would ask him in chapters 38—41. Unlike the three friends, Elihu assessed Job's problem accurately: Job's *actions* may have been right — he was not the sinner his three friends described him to be — but his *attitudes* were wrong. He was not the "saint" Job saw himself to be. Job was slowly moving toward a defiant, self-righteous attitude that was not at all healthy. It was this "know-it-all" attitude that God exposed and destroyed when He appeared to Job and questioned him.

> *"How great is God—beyond our understanding! The number of His years is past finding out"*
> *(Job 36:26).*

....

So, even though God said nothing about Elihu, the man did have a helpful ministry to Job. Unfortunately, Job wouldn't accept it.

Applying God's Truth:

1. What are some things you will *always* be able to praise God for—even when everything seems to be going wrong?

2. Can you think of anyone who has been trying—sincerely—to minister to you in some way, only to have you ignore his or her efforts? What can you do to begin to show appreciation?

3. What are some good actions you've performed lately despite an attitude that wasn't quite as good as it should have been?

DAY 28

Read **Job 38—41**

God Responds

We prefer that God speak to us in the sunshine, but sometimes He must speak out of the storm. Experiencing this majestic demonstration of God's power made Job very susceptible to the message God had for him. God's address to Job centered on His works in nature and consisted of seventy-seven questions interspersed with divine commentary relating to the question. The whole purpose of this interrogation was to make Job realize his own inadequacy and inability to meet God as an equal and defend his cause.

"Summon me, and I will answer," Job had challenged God, "or let me speak, and You reply" (Job 13:22). God had now responded to Job's challenge.

Job was sure that his speeches had been filled with wisdom and knowledge, but God's first question put an end to that delusion: "Who is this that darkens My counsel with words without knowledge?" (Job 38:2) *The Living Bible* paraphrases it, "Why are you using your ignorance to deny My providence?" God didn't question Job's integrity or sincerity; He only questioned Job's ability to explain the ways of God in the world. Job had spoken the truth about God (42:7),

> *"Then the LORD answered Job out of the storm"*
> *(Job 38:1).*

....

but his speeches had lacked humility. Job thought he knew about God, but he didn't realize how much he *didn't* know about God. Knowledge of our own ignorance is the first step toward true wisdom.

Applying God's Truth:

1. When was the last time God "spoke" to you through His nature or creation?

2. Job and his friends had debated God's will for a long time. How do you suppose they felt when God eventually began to speak for Himself?

3. If "knowledge of our own ignorance is the first step toward true wisdom," have you taken a giant step, a medium step, or a baby step? Explain.

DAY 29

Read *Job 42:1-6*

From Sinner to Servant

Job knew he was beaten. There was no way he could argue his case with God. Quoting God's very words (Job 42:3-4), Job humbled himself before the LORD and acknowledged His power and justice in executing His plans (v. 2). Then Job admitted that he had spoken about things he didn't understand (v. 3). Job withdrew his accusations that God was unjust and not treating him fairly. He realized that whatever God does is right and man must accept it by faith.

Job told God, "I can't answer Your questions! All I can do is confess my pride, humble myself, and repent." Until now, Job's knowledge of God had been indirect and impersonal, but that was changed. Job had met God personally and seen himself to be but "dust and ashes."

"The door of repentance opens into the hall of joy," said Charles Spurgeon, and it was true for Job. In the climax of the book, Job the sinner became Job the servant of God. How did Job serve God? By enduring suffering and not cursing God, and thereby silencing the devil! Suffering in the will of God is a ministry that God gives to a chosen few.

> *"Then Job replied to the Lord:*
> *'I know that You can do all things; . . .*
> *Therefore I despise myself and*
> *repent in dust and ashes"*
> *(Job 42:1-2, 6).*

Applying God's Truth:

1. When you realize you are wrong about something, how quick are you to repent?

2. In terms of percentages, how much of your own transformation from sinner to servant of God do you think is complete?

3. Do you know anyone for whom you think suffering is a "ministry"? What can you do to encourage such people?

DAY 30

Read *Job 42:7-16*

God as Author

Job ended up with twice as much as he had before. He had twenty children, ten with God and ten in his home. (He and his wife were also reunited.) Friends and relatives brought money for a "restoration fund," which Job must have used for purchasing breeders; eventually, Job had twice as much livestock as before. He was once again a wealthy man.

But we must not misinterpret this final chapter and conclude that every trial will end with all problems solved, all hard feelings forgiven, and everybody "living happily ever after." It just doesn't always happen that way! This chapter assures us that, no matter what happens to us, *God always writes the last chapter.* Therefore, we don't have to be afraid. We can trust God to do what is right, no matter how painful our situation might be.

But Job's greatest blessing was not the regaining of his health and wealth or the rebuilding of his family and circle of friends. His greatest blessing was *knowing God better and understanding His working in a deeper way.* "In the whole story of Job," wrote G. Campbell Morgan, "we see the patience of God and

> *"After Job had prayed for his friends, the LORD made him prosperous again and gave him twice as much as he had before"*
> *(Job 42:10).*

....

endurance of man. When these act in fellowship, the issue is certain. It is that of the coming forth from the fire as gold, that of receiving the crown of life" (*The Answers of Jesus to Job*, Baker, p. 117).

No matter what God permits to come into our lives, He always has His "afterword." He writes the last chapter—and that makes it worth it all.

Therefore, BE PATIENT!

Applying God's Truth:

1. Would you say that Job's story had a happy ending? Why or why not?

2. Do you think you can learn to know God better without going through the depth of suffering that Job experienced? Explain.

3. Think back to what you were suffering with as you began reading through Job. How, if at all, has your perspective changed in regard to your problems?